I0620867

The
Infinite
and
i

Jakob Muller
Mary K. Byrnes

Acknowledgments

My deepest Gratitude to God and Gurus
and to my loving Wife Mary
whose intuition has saved me so often
Thank you for your Love
and all of the people I met on my
life's journey
All photos and painting by
Artist Mary Kathryn Byrnes
Her invaluable help and Love
has made me a better Person

Jakob Muller

By Artist Wife :
Mary Kathryn Byrnes

Jakob Muller

Mary Kathryn Byrnes

4

About this Book

All poems are to help us feel

our oneness with the Creator

Thee Infinite

Read a chosen Poem three to five times

Concentrate on the Spiritual Eye

The center of Will

the point between the eyebrows

feel the response in your Heart

Let the Bliss and Truth

abide with You always

Jakob Muller

Mary Kathryn Byrnes

6

Oh Spirit Guide my Life Home
To my Infinitude in Thee, Om

Jakob Muller

Mary Kathryn Byrnes

8

In Om I live now and always, Om

Jakob Muller

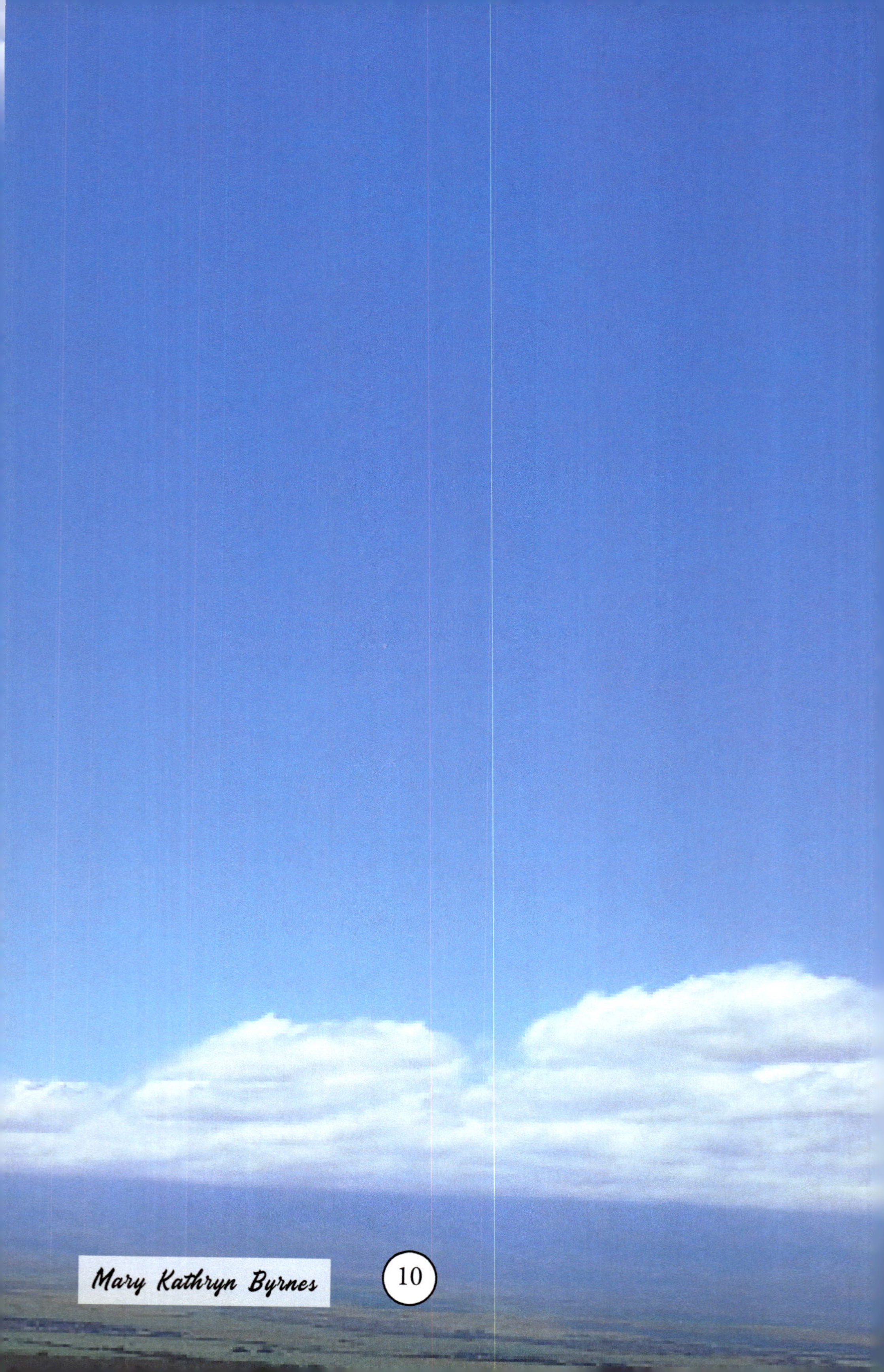
Mary Kathryn Byrnes

**Divine Mother make me bright
with Thy Light, Om**

Jakob Muller

Divine Mother awaken me into
Thy blissful Sea of Eternity, Om

Jakob Muller

Mary Kathryn Byrnes

14

Awaken within me the memory

of my Divinity, Om

Jakob Muller

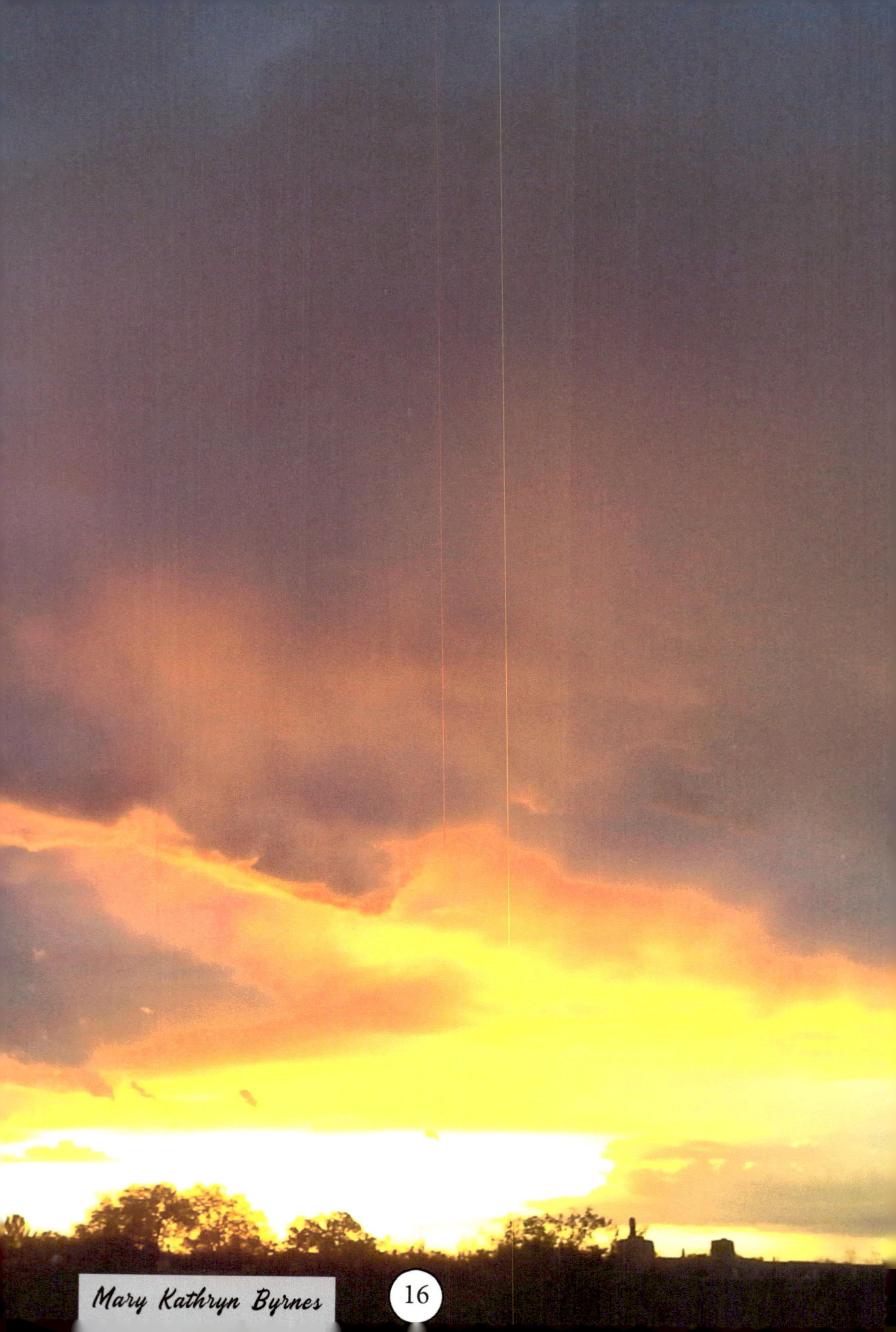

Mary Kathryn Byrnes

Divine Mother awaken me
in Thy Love, Thy Peace Thy
Presence, Om

Jakob Muller

Mary Kathryn Byrnes

18

Through my Love for Thee I Am well

Through my Love for Thee I am

redeemed, Om

Jakob Muller

Mary Kathryn Byrnes

God is my Heart

I am in the heart of God, Om

Jakob Muller

Mary Kathryn Byrnes

22

Father, receive me on Thy
Alter of Love
That I may enter Thy Temple
of Bliss, Om

Jakob Muller

Mary Kathryn Byrnes

Sacred is my Body, Mind and Soul

In Thy Arms I am forever my beloved

God, Om

Jakob Muller

Mary Kathryn Byrnes

In Thy Love I am, In Thy Presence I live

In Thy Bliss I melt, Om

Jakob Muller

Mary Kathryn Byrnes

Oh Divine Mother
Through my Love for Thee I am
healed
 I am well now and always,
Thank you God , Om

Jakob Muller

Mary Kathryn Byrnes

30

Oh God (Heavenly Father)

Awaken within me Thy

Presence and

Make me Thy Love again, Om

Jakob Muller

Mary Kathryn Byrnes

Babaji's Message. Fortitude and Endeavor

Jakob Muller

Thine is the Kingdom of Mine

Reign with me in Love divine, Om

Jakob Muller

You see Me wink if you don't think, Om

Jakob Muller

Mary Kathryn Byrnes

For my Love for Thee I am reborn
in Thee, Om

Jakob Muller

Mary Kathryn Byrnes

40

Guide me through Thy Love
to my eternal home in Thee, Om

Jakob Muller

Within Me is the river of Love

Within me is the river of Bliss

Within me is all Happiness for

Thou and I are ONE, Om

Jakob Muller

In thy heart of heart

I whisper to thee

come be with ME, Om

Jakob Muller

Mary Kathryn Byrnes

46

You are one with Me I am one with Thee

together we are the cosmic Sea, Om

Jakob Muller

Mary Kathryn Byrnes

You are my candle

I am the Light eternal illuminating the

senses with my Light of Love, bring to

Me the joy of life that I may fill thee with

my cup of Bliss, Om

49

Jakob Muller

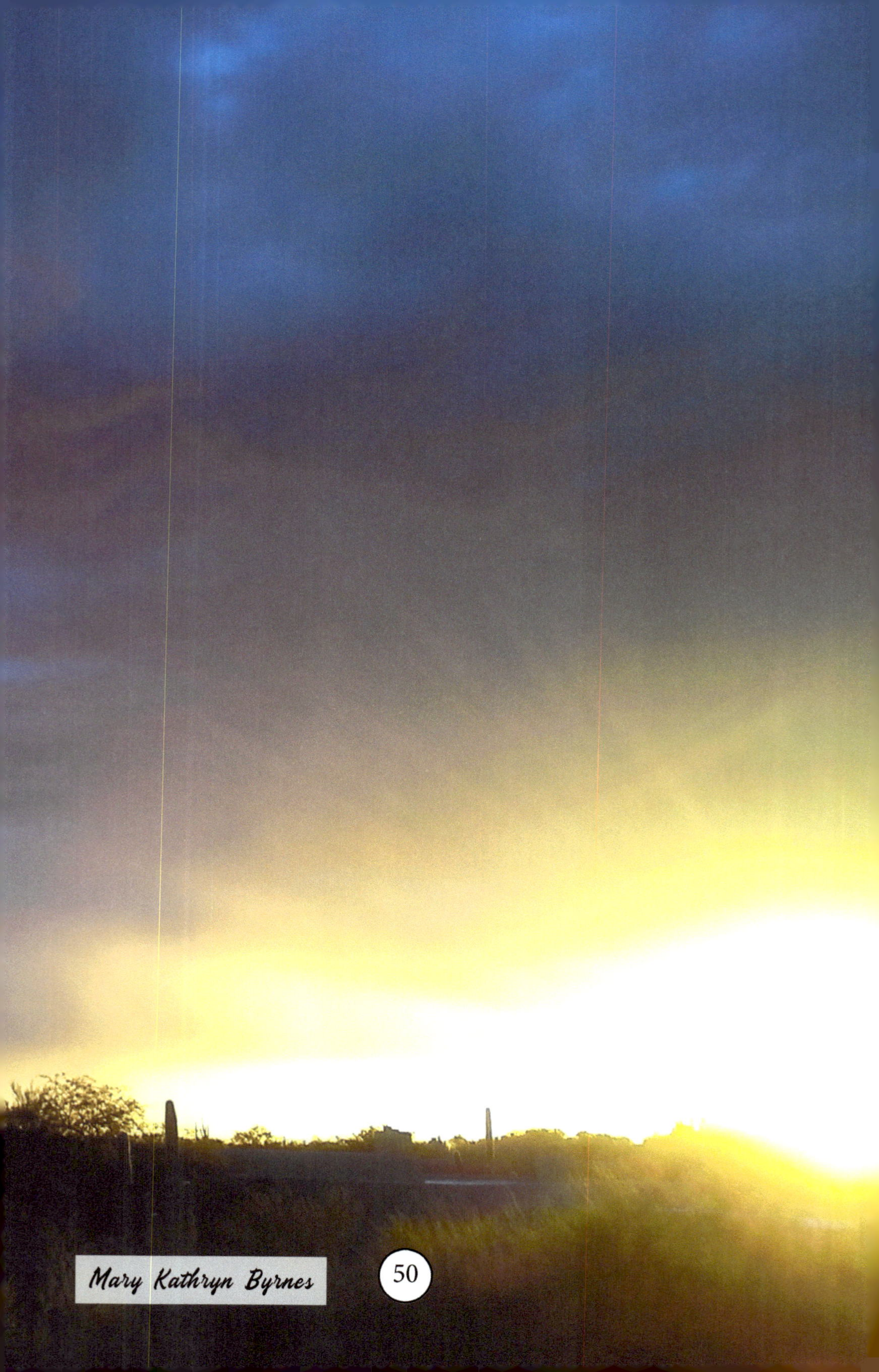

Mary Kathryn Byrnes

Everything comes, everything goes

What is in between we call Life, Om

Jakob Muller

Free yourself from the thought of

Birth and Death, you are my Infinitude

Why bother with any less,   Om

Jakob Muller

Mary Kathryn Byrnes

54

Faith is the one thing that keep us closer
for what we are.   Infinite Love, Om

Mary Kathryn Byrnes

I release thee

from now unto Eternity, may you always

Be in the light Transcendent, Om

Jakob Muller

Mary Kathryn Byrnes

Heavenly Father, evoke in me the

conciseness of Thy Sacred Presence

And may the Blessings of Thy Love

Abide with me forever, Om

Jakob Muller

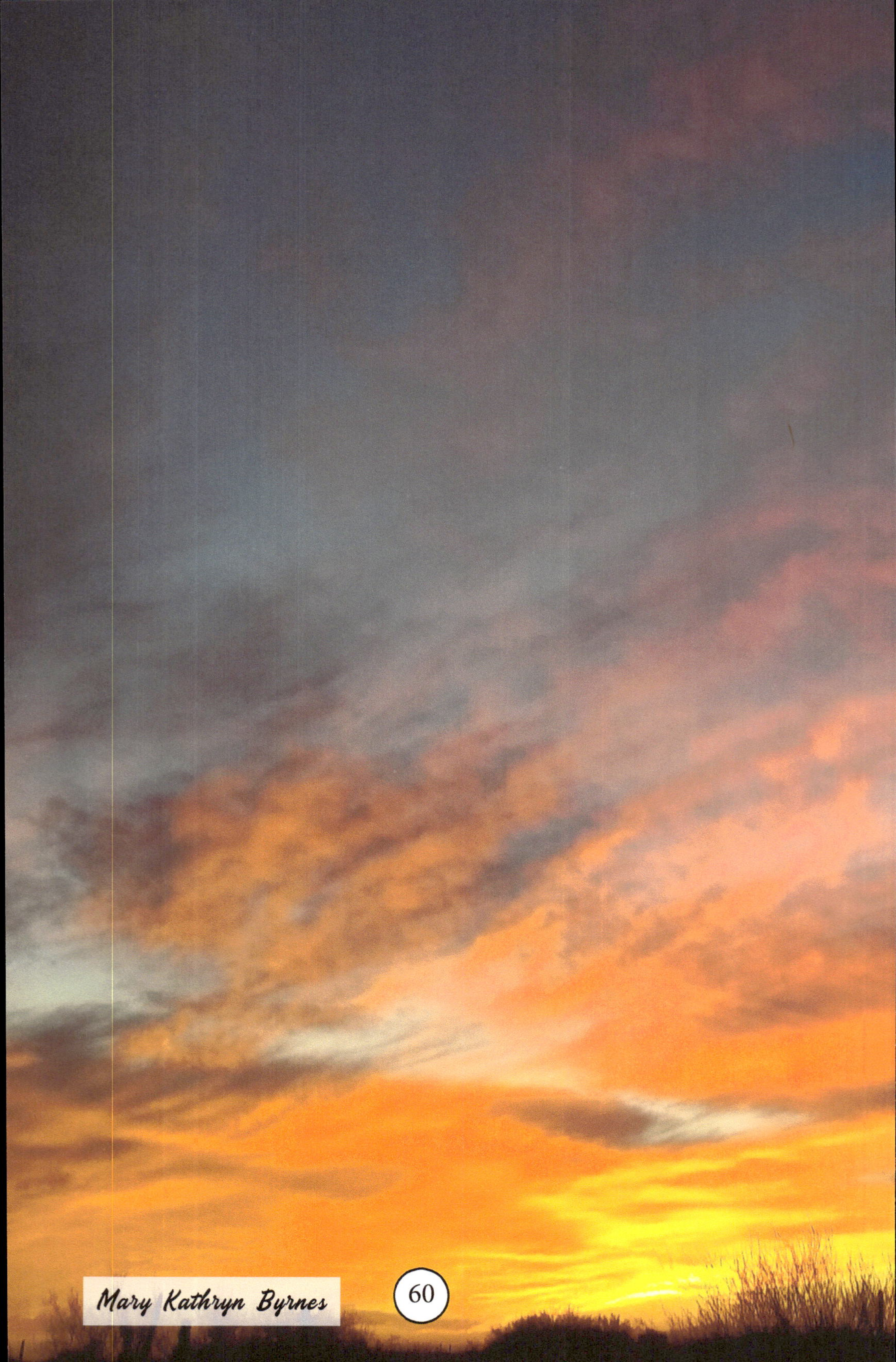
Mary Kathryn Byrnes

Your not Blood and Flesh

You are my Being of Light

Come in my Rainbow colored Heaven

Of Light and love, enjoy My Bliss filled

Cup forever. Om

Jakob Muller

Mary Kathryn Byrnes

62

Thy Breath in me my Breath in Thee

What will it be ? Om

Jakob Muller

Thou art my Light I Am thy Love. Om

Jakob Muller

Mary Kathryn Byrnes

O Christ within and without me

Awaken me to Thy Lore of Love. Om

Jakob Muller

I am Thine, you are mine

whatever YOU are I am, Om

Jakob Muller

Bread for the body, food for the Mind

Love for the Soul is the Life I extoll. Om

Jakob Muller

Make my Heart bubble with Thy Love

Make my eyes sparkle with Thy Light

Make my Soul dance with Thy Bliss

Make me feel I am Infinity in Thee. Om

Jakob Muller

Mary Kathryn Byrnes

74

Think About It !!

Free yourself from the thought

Of Birth and Death

You are you are my Infinitude

Why bother with any less, Om

Jakob Muller

Faith is the one thing that brings us closer

For what we are. Infinite LOVE. Om

Jakob Muller

Remember, the earth will go on

You must go on, with or without it, Om

Jakob Muller

Mary Kathryn Byrnes

80

Wisdom Intelligence and Will are the
Road to cosmic Imagination, Om

Jakob Muller

WISDOM

Our body is part of our expression

Rather than our Being

Mindfulness of our indwelling Presence

Is the way to inner Peace and GODDOM, Om

Jakob Muller

Mary Kathryn Byrnes

Creation is finite, Creating is infinite

Thus God exist in all forms. Om

Jakob Muller

Mary Kathryn Byrnes

86

The One of all, the One in all

The Life of all, the Love of all

is the One to Love. Om

Jakob Muller

Light is the mantle I live in and beyond it all

That is My true state of Being

You are one with me now and always, Om

Jakob Muller

Mary Kathryn Byrnes

There is no space only ME, Om

Jakob Muller

Mary Kathryn Byrnes

92

Space is the illusion of creation

Creation exists as the Phenomena

of light , Om

Jakob Muller

Mary Kathryn Byrnes

All that I am is thine

All you are is Me forever

You are the greater Self

Not the individual your playing

to be, Om

Jakob Muller

The lesson is to love all things in God

Know, that you are the Prince of the

KING, Om

Jakob Muller

Kharma is a equal measure of energy, Om

Jakob Muller

Mary Kathryn Byrnes

Truth of Being

Withdrawing in the inner Realm

No want or need for the physical

Does ever more occur

Thus the expression of being human is ended, Om

Jakob Muller

Mary Kathryn Byrnes

102

Mantel of Awareness, Creation

The journey of no return

Threshold of unlimited awareness

Super conscience Christ conscience

God conscience

When we reach the state of no want for

the physical being we enter the Pure

Or the heart of Love where all dimensions are the

Perception of the beholder. Remaining in that

State of awareness brings Enlightenment, Om

Jakob Muller

Mary Kathryn Byrnes

Those that have no Love can not hear Me

Those that have no Peace can not know Me, Om

(105)

Jakob Muller

Mary Kathryn Byrnes

106

Revere Me in everything

that lives Love Me in

everything there is, Om

Jakob Muller

Mary Kathryn Byrnes

Divine Mother,

Let The peace of Thy Love resurrect

my Life and lead me to thine eternal

home of Love, Om

Jakob Muller

Mary Kathryn Byrnes

In the Ocean of Bliss I am

In the Ocean of Love I live

In the depth of Thy Being

I am anchored forever, Om

Jakob Muller

Mary Kathryn Byrnes

In Thy heart I dream

In Thy Love I am

In Thy earth I manifest

Be Thou my Father (Mother)

The only Truth that flows through my heart

Now and always, Om

(113)

Jakob Muller

Mary Kathryn Byrnes

114

In Heaven I am In Peace I live

In Love I strive In God I am, Om

Jakob Muller

Mary Kathryn Byrnes

116

Heavenly Father

I am the floodgate of Thy prosperity

Let Thy Love Wisdom and Life

Be my expression, Om

Jakob Muller

Mary Kathryn Byrnes

In the Heart of my Father I am one

In the heart of my divine Mother I am loved

In the heart of The Infinite I am released

I am infinite now and always, Om

Jakob Muller

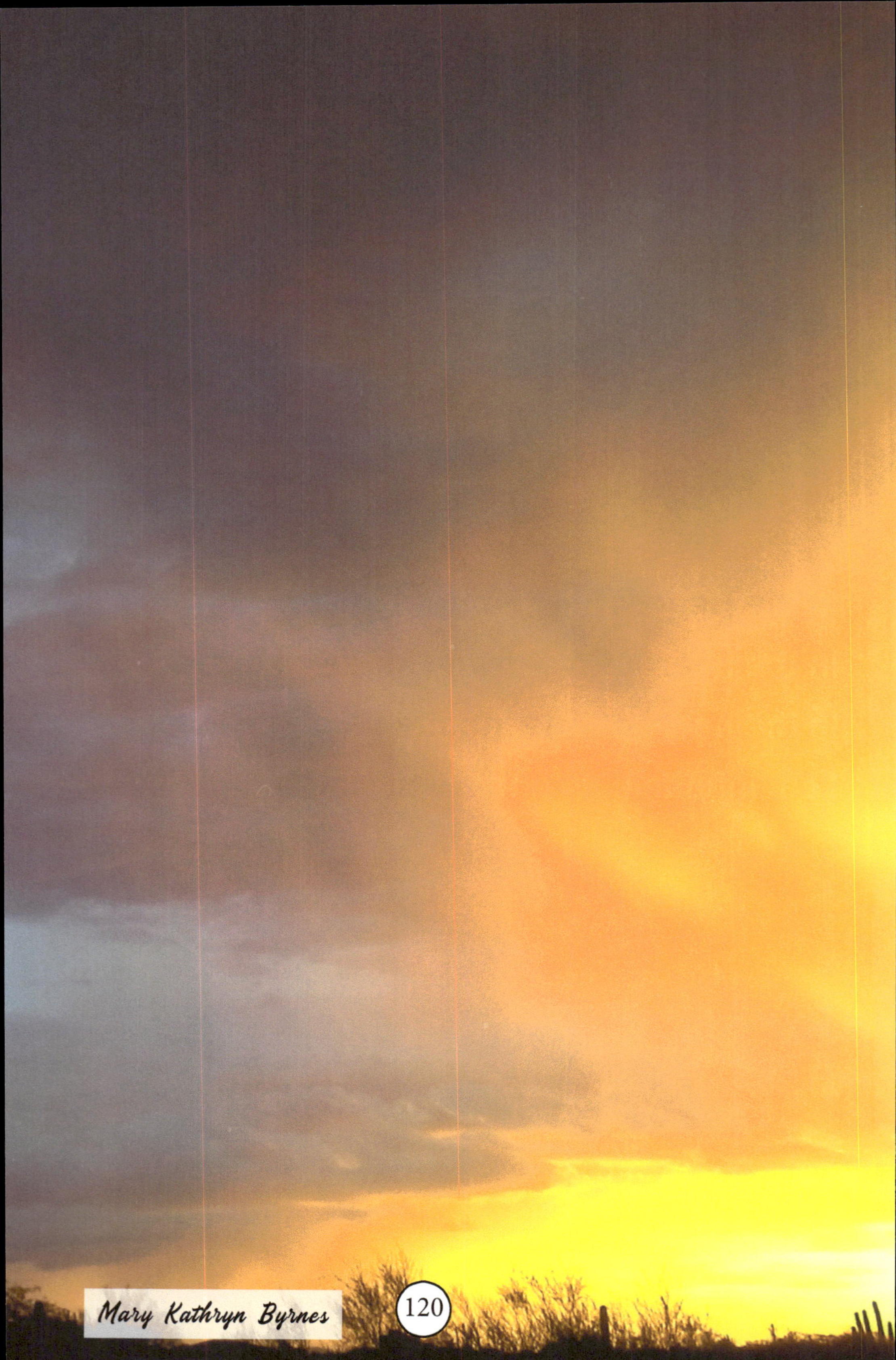

All I AM you are

All I will BE you will become

All the Love I AM you are, Om

Jakob Muller

Mary Kathryn Byrnes

122

GOD'S LOVE for us all

You are only one day old at all times

Don't look back!

Find thyself ever new in the new day

Awaken in me and see that you are me

My Prodigy ever new as I AM.   Om

Jakob Muller

In my holy Light I created thee

In my sacred Bliss I bathe thee

With my holy Love I bless thee

With my loving gifts I adorn thee

Wilt thou ever think of ME?   Om

Jakob Muller

You are me, my Life, my love

My Infinitude my all everything. Om

Jakob Muller

Mary Kathryn Byrnes

Faith is the practice of the
Remembrance of GOD. Om

Jakob Muller

Mary Kathryn Byrnes

O light of Life, O light of beauty

O light of Love, illumine my heart

with Thy presence. Om

131

Jakob Muller

Heal my eyes with the balm of Thy Love

That I may see Thy Eternity in me. Om

Jakob Muller

Mary Kathryn Byrnes

Saturated with Love and Bliss is my Soul

Saturated with Love and Bliss is my Mind

Saturated with Love and Bliss is my Body

I am a blissful Being forever. Om

Jakob Muller

INSPIRATION

I am the Wonder and Miracle of Creation

In me is the Presence of our living Father

Through his Love I am renewed

within and without. Om

Jakob Muller

Mary Kathryn Byrnes

138

OMNIPRESENCE

My eye watches over thee

My ever omnipresent Love

Always caresses thee

My blissful Sea always enfold thee

I AM always with thee in thy love

for Me. Om

Jakob Muller

Mary Kathryn Byrnes

140

Let the sunshine of my Life ever guide you

Let the Peace and my Love ever coax you

To my very Presence within you. Om

Jakob Muller

Mary Kathryn Byrnes

O God bless me with the Love
of Thine That I may see the light
of Thee in me. Om

Jakob Muller

Mary Kathryn Byrnes

Guide me through Thy
love to my eternal Home in
Thee. Om

Jakob Muller

Mary Kathryn Byrnes

For my love for Thee

I am reborn in Thee. Om

Jakob Muller

Mary Kathryn Byrnes

148

Oh Thou blue fountain of heaven open the Door of my heart and let thine all shining Omnipresence reign in our hearts minds and bodies forever. Om

149

Jakob Muller

Mary Kathryn Byrnes

150

I forgive conscientiously all
people and all creatures
That have ever offended me
wishing them the Light of
Gods love. Om

Jakob Muller

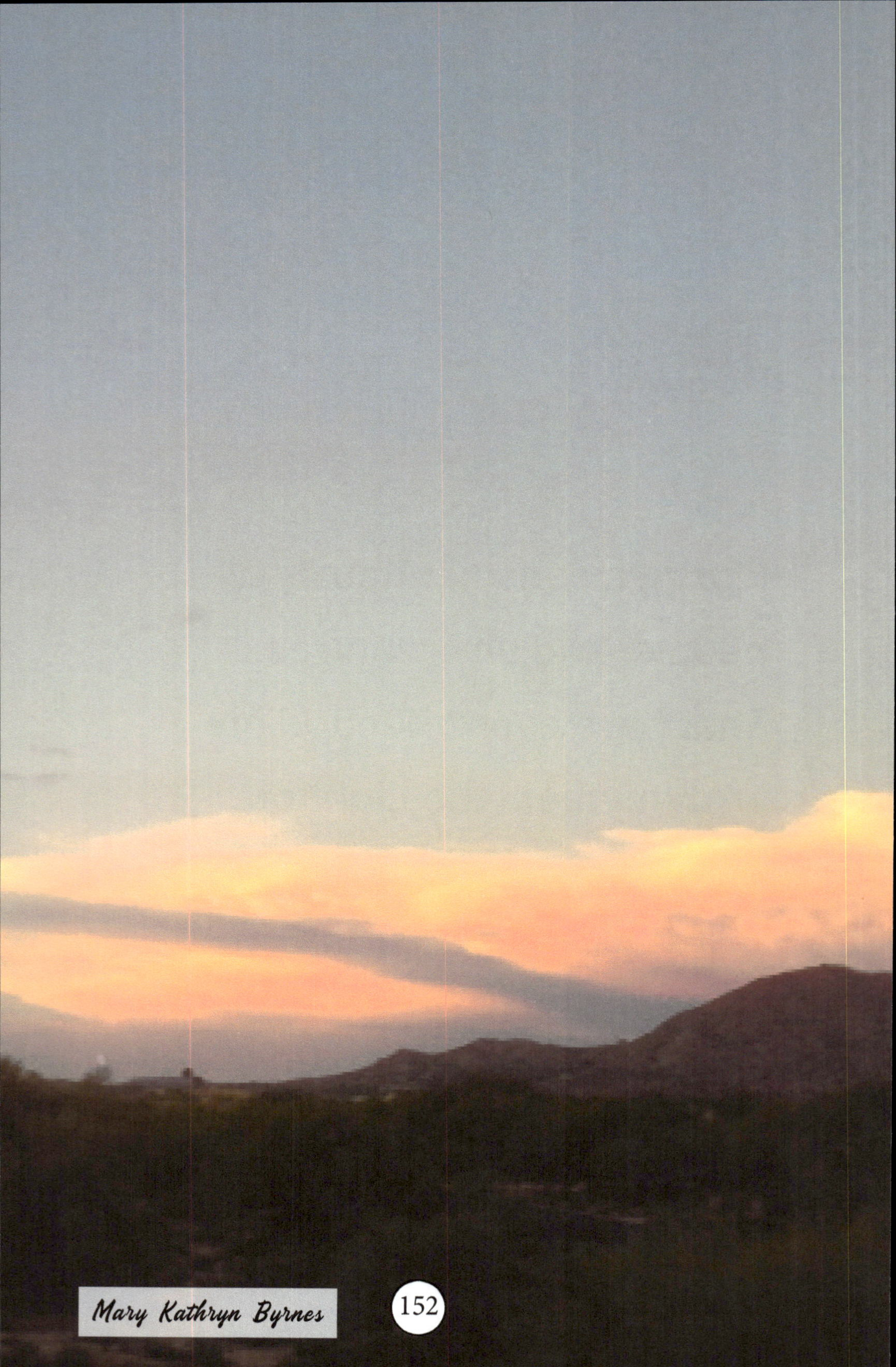

O Thou great Lover we know that
we are Powerless without Thee.
Give us of Thy Love Pure mind
and the simple but most wanted
Aspiration to seek and find Thee
in all forever Thou art mine I am
Thine forever will this Holy bond
be. Bless us. Om

Jakob Muller

Mary Kathryn Byrnes

Awareness is the key for our divine life Sweetness is the love that God has Hidden in our hearts. Om

Jakob Muller

Mary Kathryn Byrnes

All people are born with the
potential To reach Infinite
Consciousness Except few
aspire that Gift. Om

Jakob Muller

Mary Kathryn Byrnes

Ever new we are within
and without God does not
stand still…Om

Jakob Muller

Mary Kathryn Byrnes

The time has come to enjoy
life Love and the joyful
existence of being, Om

Jakob Muller

Mary Kathryn Byrnes

Then and now we find that the Ever
New is the Center of our being. The
search can never end For Oneness
will be ours. Om

Jakob Muller

Mary Kathryn Byrnes

164

And Now and Then

And now and then.......we are the one to love
And now and then.......we are the one to suffer
And now and then.......we are the one to live
And now and then.......we are the one to create
And now and then.......we are the one to become

the builder, the destroyer, the betrayed, the enemy
the lover, the truth and the forgotten, only to be ever
With the peace of All, the love of All,
the created and everlasting
Life itself. As always now, the ever and never wakeful
and ever greater increasing awareness we are seeking
and can never forget to seek, until the time fulfilled.
In that consciousness of God awareness has dissolved
our individual dreams and all dreams have become
His dream in All .....Om

Jakob Muller

Mary Kathryn Byrnes

In Thy Peace I renew myself

In Thy Love I find my Divinity

In Thy Bliss I am One with Thee, Om

Jakob Muller

Mary Kathryn Byrnes

Prayer of Protection

The Bliss of God enfolds me

The Power of God protects me

The Love of God cares for me

I am His forever Om, Om, Om

Jakob Muller

Mary Kathryn Byrnes

170

The End

www.ingramcontent.com/pod-product-compliance
Lightning Source LLC
Chambersburg PA
CBHW042239140626
46547CB00036B/23